Ladybird  Readers

Where Is My Home?

To access the audio and digital versions
of this book:

1 Go to www.ladybirdeducation.co.uk
2 Click "Unlock book"
3 Enter the code below

AWspfnzvct

Notes to teachers, parents, and carers

The *Ladybird Readers* Beginner level helps young language learners to become familiar with key conversational phrases in English. The language introduced has clear real-life applications, giving children the tools to hold their first conversations in English.

This book focuses on asking the question "Where is . . . ?" in English. It also provides practice of giving and receiving basic directions.

There are some activities to do in this book. They will help children practice these skills:

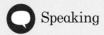 Speaking   Listening*   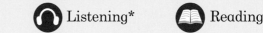 Reading

*To complete these activities, listen to the audio downloads available at **www.ladybirdeducation.co.uk**

Series Editor: Sorrel Pitts
Chants by Sorrel Pitts

LADYBIRD BOOKS

UK | USA | Canada | Ireland | Australia
India | New Zealand | South Africa

Ladybird Books is part of the Penguin Random House group of companies
whose addresses can be found at global.penguinrandomhouse.com.
www.penguin.co.uk   www.puffin.co.uk   www.ladybird.co.uk

Penguin
Random House
UK

Text inspired by *The Very Busy Spider* by Eric Carle, first published in Great Britain by Hamish Hamilton, 1985
This version first published by Ladybird Books 2024
001

Text and illustrations copyright © Penguin Random House LLC, 1984
Adapted text and artwork copyright © 2024 by Penguin Random House LLC
The moral right of the original author/illustrator has been asserted

Printed in China

The authorized representative in the EEA is Penguin Random House Ireland, Morrison Chambers, 32 Nassau Street, Dublin D02 YH68

A CIP catalogue record for this book is available from the British Library

ISBN: 978–0–241–58775–1

All correspondence to:
Ladybird Books
Penguin Random House Children's
One Embassy Gardens, 8 Viaduct Gardens, London SW11 7BW

Ladybird Readers

Where Is My Home?

Inspired by
The Very Busy Spider
by Eric Carle

"Where is my home?"
says the rooster.

"Go straight,"
says the spider.

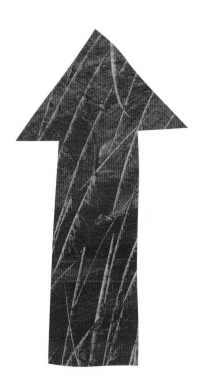

"Where is my home?"
says the cat.

"Turn left,"
says the spider.

"Where is my home?"
says the cow.

8

"Go back,"
says the spider.

"Where is my home?"
says the owl.

"Turn right,"
says the spider.

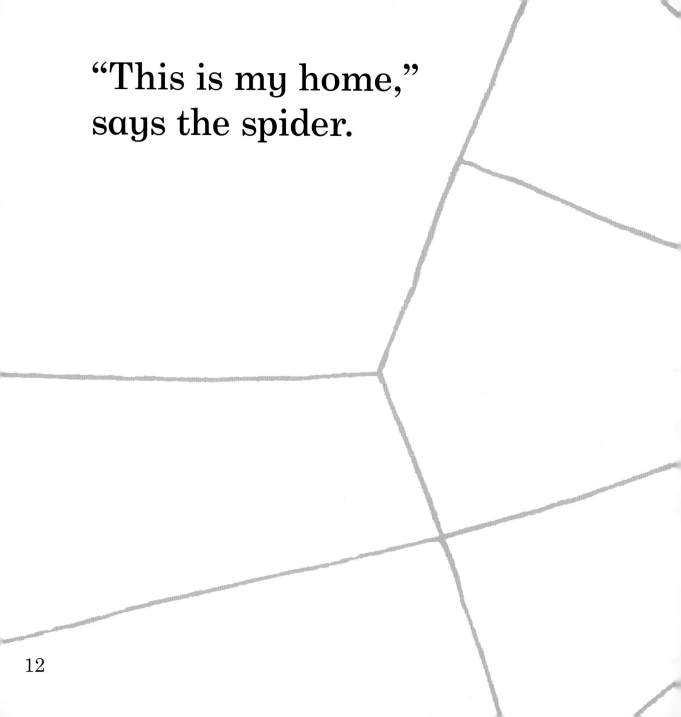

"This is my home,"
says the spider.

1 **Talk with a friend.** ⬤

Where is my home?

Turn right.

Where is my home?

Go straight.

2 **Listen. Put a** ✓ **by the correct words.**

1 a "I am an owl." ✓

  b "I am a cat."

2 a "Where is my home?"

  b "This is my home."

3 a "Turn left."

  b "Turn right."

4 a "Go straight."

  b "Go back."

3 Read and clap!

Where is my home, home, home?
Go straight, straight, straight!

Where is my home, home, home?
Turn left, left, left!

Where is my home, home, home?
Go back, back, back!

Where is my home, home, home?
Turn right, right, right!

Where is my home, home, home?
This is my home!